Raintree is an imprint of Capstone Global Library Limited, a company incorporated in England and Wales having its registered office at 264 Banbury Road, Oxford, OX2 7DY – Registered company number: 6695582

www.raintree.co.uk
myorders@raintree.co.uk

Edited by Erika L. Shores
Designed by Ashlee Suker
Picture research by Marcie Spence
Production by Eric Manske

ISBN 978 1 4747 1902 5
20 19 18 17 16 15
10 9 8 7 6 5 4 3 2 1

Photo Credits
Alamy Images: blickwinkel, 21; Shutterstock: AGphotographer, 13, alek.k, 9, basketman23, 17, Elenamiv, design element, Jane Rix, 7, Kookkai_nak, design element, Linda Armstrong, 19, Phillip W. Kirkland, 15, Simon Krzic, 11, tepic, cover, 1, verityjohnson, 5

We would like to thank Gail Saunders-Smith, PhD, and Dr. Celina Johnson for their invaluable help in the preparation of this book.

Every effort has been made to contact copyright holders of material reproduced in this book. Any omissions will be rectified in subsequent printings if notice is given to the publisher.

All the internet addresses (URLs) given in this book were valid at the time of going to press. However, due to the dynamic nature of the internet, some addresses may have changed, or sites may have changed or ceased to exist since publication. While the author and publisher regret any inconvenience this may cause readers, no responsibility for any such changes can be accepted by either the author or the publisher.

Note to Parents and Teachers

This book describes and illustrates cows. The images support early readers in understanding the text. The repetition of words and phrases helps early readers learn new words. This book also introduces early readers to subject-specific vocabulary, which is defined in the Glossary section. Early readers may need assistance to read some words and to use the Table of contents, Glossary, Read more, Internet sites and Index sections of the book.

Printed and bound in China.

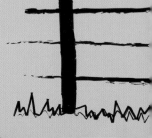

Contents

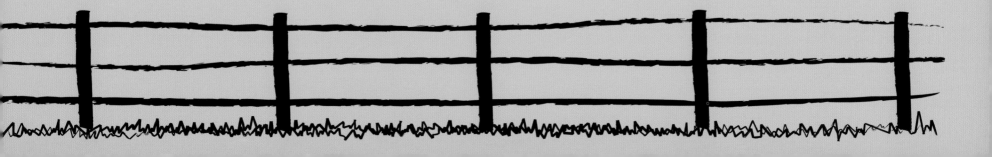

Meet the cows

Moo! It's early morning
on the farm. Here come
some spotted cows!
They walk on hoofs
and swish their tails.

Cows have wide muzzles
and big ears. Cows have
short or long hair that is black,
white, brown, red or grey.
Some cows are spotted.

Dairy cows weigh about 680 kilogrammes (1,500 pounds). That's as heavy as two motorbikes!

Grazing days

Cows eat grass, hay

and grain. Cows burp up

their swallowed food as cud.

Cows chew the cud

for eight hours a day.

A cow drinks 114 litres

(30 gallons) of water every day.

That's enough to fill a bath.

Cows drink from ponds,

streams or tanks.

New life

A calf is born! It stands up

within 30 minutes.

It's an adult after one year.

Cows can live for

15 to 20 years.

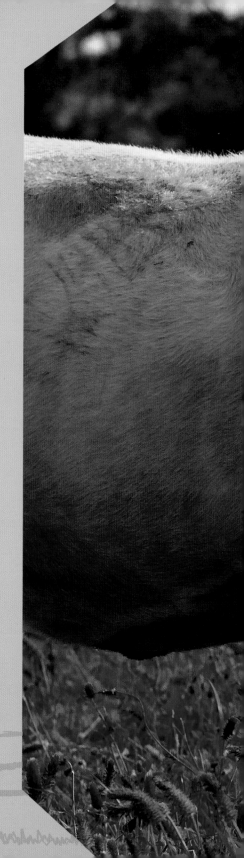

On the farm

Cows raised for their milk

are called dairy cows.

They are milked in a milking parlour.

Machines pump milk from

the cows' udders.

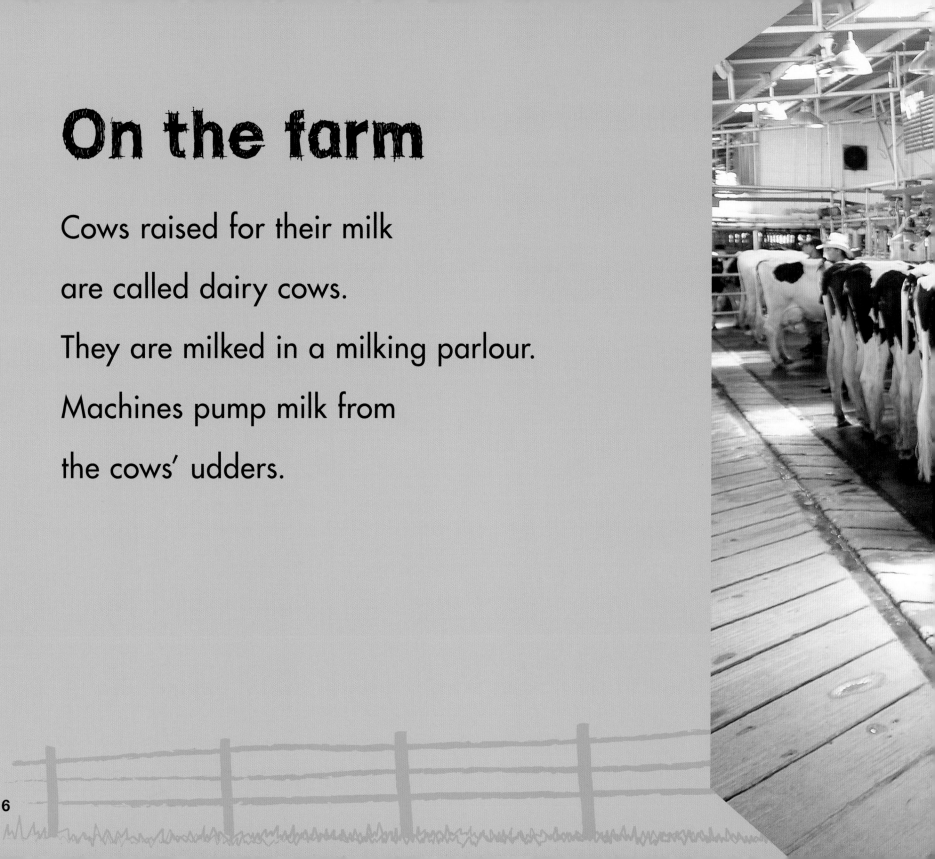

udder

Beef cows are raised for meat.

Their hides are used to

make shoes, leather jackets

and many other products.

Cows might sleep in barns

when it's very cold, hot

or stormy. They snooze

in grassy areas called pastures

the rest of the time.

Glossary

cud swallowed food that is burped back into a cow's mouth and chewed again

dairy cow female cow that produces milk

grain plant seeds such as barley, corn, oats and wheat

graze eat grass

hay dried grass used to feed cows

hoof cow's foot

muzzle nose, mouth and lower part of a cow's face

pasture grassy area of land that cows and other animals feed upon

udder body part that fills with milk and hangs under a cow

Read more

Farm Animals (Say & Point Picture Book), Nicola Tuxworth (Armadillo Books, 2015)

Farm Animals: True or False? (True or False?), Daniel Nunn (Capstone Raintree, 2013)

Journey of a Glass of Milk (Journey of A..), John Malam (Heinemann Library, 2013)

Websites

discoverykids.com/category/animals/
Learn facts about animals and check out photos of all sorts of animals on this website.

kids.nationalgeographic.com/animals
Search for different sorts of animals and learn where they live, what they eat and more.

Index